The Dedalus Press

Spring in Henry Street

Eva Bourke

SPRING IN HENRY STREET

EVA BOURKE

DEDALUS

The Dedalus Press
24 The Heath,
Cypress Downs,
Dublin 6W
Ireland

© 1996 Eva Bourke / The Dedalus Press

ISBN 1 873790 90 2 (paper)
ISBN 1 873790 91 0 (bound)

Cover painting by Benjamin de Burca

Acknowledgement is made to:
Poetry Ireland Review, Cyphers, The Honest Ulsterman, Aquarius, Stet, The Cúirt Journal, The Padraic Fallon Anthology, The Living Landscape Anthology, UCG Women's Studies Centre Review. The poem "Goat" was commissioned for an exhibition of paintings and poems organised by Poetry Ireland.

Dedalus Press Books are represented and distributed abroad by Password, 23 New Mount St., Manchester M4 4DE.

Printed in Ireland by Colour Books Ltd.

The Dedalus Press receives financial assistance from An Chomhairle Ealaíon, The Arts Council, Ireland.

CONTENTS

Door	9
Song, be my Friendly Asylum!	11
A Tree doesn't know it is miserable ...	12
What My Love Likes Doing	15
Mother of Eros	17
Penelope	20
Love after Chagall	22
Love after Gabrielle d'Estrées & her Sister	23
Temptations	24
The Annunciation	25
Infinitesimal Calculus	29
Backyards, Interiors	30
You want to control your sky	32
The Day You Come	33
When You Arrive in Your Exile Shoes	34
Spring in Henry Street	39
What Happened to Mlle Bourienne?	41
To the Distributor of Souls	44
Permissive Days	51
Not a Poem about writing Poetry	53
Goat	55
Glasgow Aubade	63
Summer near Auvers	65
From *Correspondence Secrète*	66
The Scrap Dealer's Report	69
Reading Hikmet in Connemara	71
Trip to an Island	74

On his deathbed, a man of vineyards spoke into Marcela's ear. Before dying he revealed his secret:

"The grape," he whispered, "is made of wine".

Marcela Pérez-Silva told me this, and I thought: If the grape is made of wine, then perhaps we are the words that tell who we are.

Eduardo Galeano
The Book of Embraces

DOOR

Turn the key and you'll hear the echoes
in a room beside the sea
where a family have just packed up and left;
the floorboards surge underfoot,
all windows are awash with emptiness.

Close it and it'll lead you away from sunken worlds,
out of a dark ocean's corridors
where sharks nose around its doorstep
and administrators count the small change
in the pockets of the drowning.

You'll come upon it in high walls opening on trees
writing their slow names into the sky
above expanses of water
flashing back the latest run-down
of their peace talks with the wind.

The faded greens of summer houses, onion domes
are on loan from it,
and if you follow it into the outskirts
where a child in red swings
back and forth on a gate,

you will see the light around her tremble
with green overtones.
Step through it into darkness
and listen to the night's deep bell,
its sustained chime.

The sentries by the portal dream on soft thresholds.
At times when walls become doorless
and all escape routes are barred,
how could you live
without these consolations?

SONG, BE MY FRIENDLY ASYLUM!

Friedrich Hölderlin

Blue the road
beneath a wilderness of sky,
clouds, flocks of birds –
not to know where I am going,
the road high and blue,

and I never ask
where does it lead to?

I stretch out
on thresholds,
in doorways;
the smell of lavender
is my cushion;

wanderer,
with nothing but the blue word
hope in my pocket.

A tree doesn't know it is miserable ...

Pascal

A green dome
in treeless country:
the graveyard at Menlo.

I first saw a heron
sit motionless there
for hours.

The wind plays barber
to the beeches,
clips their crowns.

Between lake and plains
trees point to
the sky's altitude.

Trees are constant negotiators:
roots firmly in the ground, they write
their slow signatures into the sky.

If you lose your way
near the sea
follow the inlandpointing trees.

When the deluge receded
Noah discovered the arc
was moored to the top of an olive tree.

First step in dreaming:
sleep under a tree's
dark and dazzling canopy.

Second step:
let your dreams build nests
among its leaves.

Third step:
let trees teach you
how not to know you're miserable.

On the tightly-
knit branches
young crows perform cartwheels.

The words *sycamore*
sassafras acacia
sway and rustle.

The words *chain-saw*
power-tool axe
shriek and thud.

To protect the lovely Daphne
the gods changed her
into a laurel tree

but their best gift was to Philemon and Baucis:
to become a lime and an oak
standing side by side forever.

Trees caress every breeze
with thousands
of fingers.

At storm time they have
powerful leanings
towards each other.

The poet Hikmet was a nut tree
in an Istanbul Park:
neither his beloved nor a policeman noticed.

In the Garden of Eden
(Anonymous, Cologne 1485)
even the cherry trees make love.

My thoughts like flocks
of starlings chattering
in the crown of the neighbour's ash tree.

The elder at the end of the garden:
in summer it is all
for the birds.

In autumn it is festooned
with cobwebs,
spiders' mock suns.

Among trees
the most haunting music
is played on wind instruments.

But sometimes if you listen closely
there is also
the most perfect silence.

WHAT MY LOVE LIKES DOING

Long avenues, avenidas crossing waterways,
a little drunk around
a star-shaped square,
he takes the sinking gold into his hands
on what was once a sober elm-lined place
(and gladly lets the pedants take offence

who gather channels by the twos and threes,
make rivers run the gauntlet
of low iron bridges,
who square the roots of houses, belltowers, trees
and waste no time deciphering the cat-
calls from the laughing stalls and galleries.)

He sings the blues and greens along the way.
Such multitude, such drinking
at the overflowing tap!
He'd have us dance on floral domes of clay
and punch-drunk skip on oceans without sinking.
(And never mind the things the experts say.)

The multitude, the wines, the coloured glass.
(What pauperism of the mind
that only counts and classifies!)
How could you count each cloud, or grass by grass?
My love alone accounts for double-bind
of bodies, arms and fingers, lips and eyes.

He likes to paint the night sky bright and umber
and drink the sinking gold
in little elm-lined places.
Avenidas slip like starfish through our slumber,
our brains, our hair, our hands and moonstruck faces.
What pulls this river to the coasts of summer?

MOTHER OF EROS

She's lost among the trivia collected,
bills, headaches, heartaches, disconnected
phone calls, postcards from forgotten places,
hopeless letters full of cautious phrases
like 'nice to see you sometime' and 'when
you pass through here, do call again',
but can't think for the life of her which 'here',
the writer's signature's become a blur;
she treads so lightly, watching cracks with care,
keeps to a thin line, counts each greying hair,

she pins a smile on for each face she meets,
she talks about the cold, she feels it so, she greets
endearments in a language long deferred
with every kind of frosty effort, in a word
she's lost all nerve and thinks that all despise
her, gauche and unwanted, with her tired vice
of putting on a false front that belies
the *cris de cœur*, the tears, the drugs, the booze.
It's omissions and cold routine that kill
the frozen months of Januaries, Februaries till

a March that thaws and flowers seems just a blunder
of seasons bent on getting on with it. But under
the iced-up weeks, notes of dismissal, dates
not kept and messages not replied to stir
the plosive sounds of pulp and peach and pear,
for laid out in silkpaper-cushioned crates,
net-covered like old gentlewomen's faces,
rest these univalves, ripe ovaries in their juices.
And like a somnambulist that's being led
I want to take her down the length of Henry Street

into the tranquil darkness of a shed
that's lined with shelves of every type of fruit
where this comfortable woman moves, with apple head,
ample arms, in striped, open-necked shirt.
This is a neighbourhood garden of paradise,
not just some vegetable shop, she presides
over an unseasonal summer of tastes. She'll call
us past bags of onions, spuds and swedes,
the earth-bound care-takers of our needs,
into her inner sanctum where with all

the sly bravura, the relish of the gourmande,
she picks from varied piles luxuriant
outlandish things, hands us, maybe a mango,
to taste its blushing flesh with total sang-froid
and then demands to know how we'd describe
the jungle tangs beneath its smooth cool endocarp.
For years we've been at naming games together,
test uglies, lychees, kumquats, puckered leather
bags of granadills for the lip-closing labials,
they yield a serpent's sting of graded vowels,

from jujube, pampelmousse, to pippin, passion fruit,
the hushed-up sibilants, the glottal stops
of pleasure, honey dew melons flattened at the tops
like planets, plums and cherries full of sweet blood,
tangerine, pineapple, pawpaw, papay,
we say it over and again like a lullaby,
and harshness softens and the ice gives way,
as morning peels the rind of night from day,
as tongues that tell sweetness from bitterness
repeating palatals of yes and yes and yes

and the aspirates of an entire phonetic
of heaven and heart and him and her, the erotic
richness we find on pulling back the skin
on the secret luscious flesh within,
hidden like feelings, segments, pips and drupes,
the pod-bags, scent-bags, clustered seeds, the globes,
and like a sudden miracle, the neat
geometry of the Chinese lantern fruit
sheltering inside its hexagonal tapered sphere
the acid burning flame of Demeter.

And last but not least she unearths from her trove
pomegranates, the archetypal fruit of love,
whose scarlet seeds are tightly parcel-packed
in vellum-wrap and spill out as the cracked
shell of the broken world-egg once let spill
out all creation, earth and sea and sky,
the shell to which the goddess hoists her sail
to skim an ocean of milk. Moon-mother stand by
her, Danae, all-giver, open your jar
of grains and fruit, Mother of Eros – help her.

PENELOPE

At night when watchmen and dogs are asleep
and the suitors lie in a stupor
from too much Attic wine,

Penelope is in her workshop amid shuttles and spools
picking up threads where she left them
the day before.

Colourful yarns pile up around her
as the shuttle moves backwards
and shapes dissolve under her hands:

Lovers rise from the grass, go their separate ways,
baskets empty themselves of fruit,
trees leave the orchards,

sunlight lifts from hills as orchards and hills, too, vanish,
a melody plays back to its keynote,
a faun unstrings his lyre.

Sometimes she feels she is holding the fabric
of the world she fears
she, too, might undo if she's not careful.

But before twilight she has come to the last
length of red thread which she pulls
from her weft:

Arrows fly back into quivers, a small stocky old man
shoulders his bow and leaves through the courtyard,
Telemachus lowers his dripping sword,

hands unclench, wounds close, blood re-enters the heart,
the suitors arise with desire
in their glances

at herself who, grown old and sad at her loom,
selects colours and yarns,
begins from scratch.

LOVE AFTER CHAGALL

At night all cities are Paris:
a gentle red bull lowing at the sky
on the Place de la Concorde.

All nightskies are divided
into blues and greens above the Marmara Sea:
crescent and star.

A young woman
enters from the right
cradling a dove:

my head is turned inside out to you
whose body gleams white with plumage –
you lift and spread me like wings.

Love after Gabrielle d'Estrées and her Sister

(School of Fontainebleau)

Our bodies are continents our hands
have often travelled and know by heart:
deltas, plains, rolling hills,
every fault line and outcrop.

Day or night in tandem they find their way,
know about mean temperatures,
are familiar with sudden storms
and periods of extreme calm.

Eyes in every fingertip they explore
the rough and smooth places,
pick and choose the hot spots,
glacial deposits and wiry undergrowths.

Our bodies, not yet
broken up and drifted apart,
chaste and maculate
in the surf of their separate darknesses.

TEMPTATIONS

(Flemish 1478)

start as snakes will start discreetly
    only make the grass tips move
        sleep in beech shade

dream of avenues
    flanked by palaces
        dream of technicolour empires

guard crowns and mitres
    and guard with special care
        the hearts of nightingales

from a faint hum in telegraph poles
    from slight atmospheric disturbances
        gather data on the perfidy of angels

leave nothing behind you except
    a few winding tracks in the sand
        a sloughed-off skin

THE ANNUNCIATION

I

Colonies of pigeons on sills and parapets,
all the cornices or ledges serve as altitude-drops,
take-off points or landing strips
and everywhere the grain-coloured façades are streaked
with pigeon shit, delicate splashes of anthracite,
pearl-grey, bluish-grey, chalk-white,
as abstract and patterned as an action painter's canvas;
the Palazzo Pubblico with its formal rows
of hollow roof bricks, the slender campanile above all
the scallop-shaped piazza at the heart
of the city, all is pigeon territory, pigeon-soiled
and everywhere there's the flutter, the rustle of folding
or spreading wings, a furtive bustle of cooing
or tripping back and forth,
an indefinable activity, officious as a host of angels
or a secret police force intent on some mysterious
and terrible business;
the birds' short fat necks ripple
with metallic tints, steel-blues, greens,
their heads nod and tick and tick
from side to side as they peck the ground or fix
everything and nothing with indifferent
or strangely observant eyes – you wouldn't know which –

and now, just as ever, ragazzi do their peacock strut
across the square, around its curvilinear top
over ornamental tiles fanning out from the city hall entrance,
the gravel of pigeon feed crunching underfoot;
the boys move through hovering flocks,
flocks taking off at a whim;
one bird settles awkwardly on someone's hand,
a little puffed-up with self-importance it eyes
the admiring audience, our children, who clearly feel
this takes some bravado, some *savoir-faire* with birds;
badly poised, using its wings for balance
it steadies its plump body
on this most unsteady of landing places.
This is birdland, pigeon dominion,
and we – seated in Benedetto's cafe
in the late autumn sun –
feel outlandish and on sufferance
among the muted golds and reds of this town,
tourists, pedestrians, land-bound, with pockets
full of mementoes, address books, unfinished
letters, useless currencies.
Feathers drift and sail to earth
like huge snowflakes.

II

O painters of Val d'Arbia working to the end
of daylight grouping lilies, peacocks
and the ever-present doves
around the feet of a sullen young girl
who's just had very disquieting news –

in spite of the courtly richness of her dress
she turns halfway suppliantly towards five or six angels
opening their goose-quill wings
in the shimmering blue above her like shears.

III

On Monte Oliveto where the monks keep a three star
restaurant and flocks of fan-tail doves,
their little fast Fiat cars
set out at all times of the day, in twos
and threes the monks fly up
and down the hilly streets like white hooded birds;
one of the birdmen takes us under his wing, his skirts
rustle and flutter, he coos and beckons,
throws hemp seed into the courtyard
and the doves come down in one noisy go
a flurry of plumage and flapping
as though they are completely out of their trees,
and for a moment we are encloistered
in the roar of a wind-tunnel.
San Benedetto loved birds, says the birdmonk, and true
enough, all along the cloister walls in Sodoma's
frescoes, birds of all description, even the odd owl,
crowd around the rotund Saint's feet rubbing shoulders
with frogs, snails, bats, foxes;
our guide sports a growth on his forehead
the size and shape of a dove egg covered in sallow skin
as smooth as egg shell.

IV

We have rented a house on Poggio del'Amore,
the Hill of Love, which we share with a screech owl;
it sleeps in the attic through the daylight
hours, emerges some time after dark announcing
its coming with a long drawn-out savage shriek,
so heart-chilling, triumphant,
wild with joy, that every living
thing on the hill trembles and holds its breath
and creeps deeper into the shadows, unseen
it streaks past the open windows
through gathering October fog
and vanishes among olive trees, cypresses
and shrubs of the valley, and often,
jolted out of first sleep, I lie awake
fighting the return of my usual
nocturnal demons until dawn
transforms the fog into layered, shimmering fabrics
their gauze-like edges running with blues,
peacock-blue, cyanin, *taubenblau*
and the owl returns with the same fierce cry
and slips to rest between rafters and roof tiles.
There is no reprieve, it tells me,
there is no reprieve.

INFINITESIMAL CALCULUS

Through the panes of the first floor window the world looks like a graph-sheet neatly divided into 24 squares. Only somewhere in the infinite, so I'm told, do parallels converge. Sometimes birds, starlings or seagulls, fly past in rising or falling curves or describe a semi-circle with a very wide radius, tangential to a rooftop or an aerial. I have no idea of the geometry of flight. In the falling curve of ever-sameness from day to day a neighbour is polishing the brass knocker on her front door. In the rising curve of the fresh-leaved privet hedge several young sparrows are testing their new wings. In the semi-circle of anguish an ambulance passes by. All ambulances travelling parallel on the same plane and at the same speed will converge in the infinite. This one might turn back before it's too late, just as the writing on its front reads in reverse. Only inside us dwell things that are not reversible. But in dreams they can be. Last night I dreamed the dead were still alive and I solved the sky's equation. On today's overcast graph-sheet it is insoluble and y and x equal nothing on earth.

BACKYARDS, INTERIORS

Pieter de Hooch, 1629 – 1684

"Oblique light on the trite ... "
Derek Mahon, <u>Courtyards in Delft</u>

The light is autumnal between back wall
lean-to roof and arched gate;
the little that can be seen of the sky
above a fuzz of clouds is of that blue
recalling wet blue sheets pegged up to dry.

The viewer's eye is firmly guided down
to earth, to ochre yard tiles,
worn smooth by comings and goings
and still damp from a recent gush of water;
the bucket beside the birch broom,

rimmed with glistening drops,
takes up the motif of light again
in this otherwise half-lit backyard,
but the startling indigo of the woman's skirt
(the one standing on the outhouse steps

holding her daughter's hand)
is like a variation of the sky on a deeper note,
or the onrush of a second theme
in this meticulously composed *symphonie domestique,*
or a sudden change from minor to major.

Is all this trite? Who's to say whether the girl in the lane
leaning against the maroon and white
brick facing of the archway
is waiting for her man to come home
or – arms akimbo – preparing for departure,

taking a last look? Although at first
the sense of confined space is stifling,
there are doors flung open, windows
letting in the sun, vistas of canals
where eventually ships, tugs, trawlers must pass by.

Where, if they're going, will these women go?
How far? The carved gilt frame?
Or will they – one mild autumn day – break out
of the confines of portraiture, crack through layers of paint,
disrupt the composition?

One woman rises from having searched for lice
in her daughter's hair,
tucks up her pinafore and starts
to pack a wicker basket.
She places a pistol beneath her linen shirts

while her little girl hits
a puck across the polished floor tiles:
her story will be told on a different panel,
already the colours have been rubbed and mixed
with linseed oil, the canvas is prepared.

You want to control your sky

You want to control you sky
keep it from touching another

your moon
from crossing any airspace but yours

you pile brick on brick
man your observation towers round the clock

but birds can't be controlled
they fly past your barricades

lazy clouds sail
over your check-points

at breakfast lizards from abroad
are sunning themselves on your ramparts

warm breezes waft across to you
carrying orchard scents

someone has been busy
cracking your sad wintry codes

your no-man's land is going to seed with flowers
and since this morning

white flags have appeared
on the thornbushes of your lanes.

THE DAY YOU COME

The day you come take me
in taxis full of music
preferably Jazz

take me to waterfronts let
boys in white untie
crafts fluttering buntings

go starboard with me go fishing
let's have the catch of the year
cool bodies in sequins and yards of sail

let's cruise to islands where green
speaks in tongues
and the evenings gild hallways

where rooms step beyond
their windows in lazy drapes
of beaded muslin

we'll listen to the green
speaking of tongues
converse with blackbirds

lift roofs to the moon
complete with cat-families
and song

When you arrive in your exile shoes

When you arrive in your exile shoes,
your foreign sandals,
walk over the seven bridges of this town
without crossing one twice,
if you don't know the language ask for the way
get lost in circles slide
your hand along bridge walls
polished to marble by thousands before you.

Let your heart go
let it go back and forth between words,
cross bridges of words that have no foundations,
spanning nothing but darkness.
Let it become a traveller in words,
send it out to search among syllables,
prepare it to find not one
it could call home.

Let it go to the heron for help
who polices the river's edge,
folded in upon herself she stands
ragged as an old parasol,
now and again suddenly tests
the lightning-quick serpentine strike
of her long neck
then returns to her pose of motionless cipher.

Question the moorhen's oracle –
she's alien here too
with her shellack beak she fiercely patrols
her nest among reeds – then swing
upwards and along the great waterway
downstream where the cormorant harangues
families of fish and downstream
he flies in his dripping wild plumage
never yielding his secret.

Head for the river's mouth –
perhaps you'll find there a sound familiar as bread
or a sentence alive with the smells of childhood,
a word like wax, yeast or grass,
a word that lies in your palm
smooth and round as a pebble.

The river has news of the Nile, the Amazon,
brings inland gifts
of black earth and eels to the sea,
deposits a soft silt in the bay
where hundreds of swans glide and mull
over the estuary's ground
bending their bewitching necks
to the mystery of their reflections.

Decode the sea road's surprise turns
past reclaimed breakwater secured swamplands
kept a haughty eye on by Fosset's circus camel
who strides the boundaries curling her lip
at a brown man and a flowerlike woman in silks.
Salute them,
then come into the open and shelter
below the sky's tattered awnings
by a gigantic water-snake that spits out
screaming children under yellowing glass roofs.

Ah, the grand hotels festooned with their glad
rags and the face-lifting arcades
flushed neon-pink
dreamy-eyed boys fight star wars
and women with winning ways count their full houses,
behind submarine windows party-men
switched on to dancing mode
are stepping it out in the clubs;
if you trespass here watch out,
below gilt façades and upwardly mobile developments
instant snap-shooters will hand you
double negatives of yourself
you won't recognise or understand.

Then turn back,
back to the easy-come easy-go town
with its grey walls and luminous clock-face,
its angels' hellos and farewells,
where the rain perpetually speaks
its received incomprehensible language,

tenderly combs the hair of gables,
the hair of bin-collectors,
of milkmen on the delivery round,
of milk cartons stacked outside newspaper shops,
combs alike the hair of schoolgirls all in maroon,
the hair of dead elms,
of angelus bells announcing and announcing,
of the river tearing at the bridge posts,
the hair of the cathedral, three triangles and one spire,
the hair of graveyards,
of chimney pots and derelict houses,
the hair of the Mermaid Fishmongers,
the hair of the shuttered post office,
the hair of the drowned,
the hair of the living,
the hair of exiles listening for answers
in the rain's repetitive small-talk –

and the rain will comb your hair tenderly
with thousands of fingers.

Along the shore the rocks maintain a stony silence
and with many sighs the tide combs and parts,
parts and combs their mingled green and brown hair.
The lighthouse in its striped beachboy gear
keeps repeating itself
on the topic of danger, till dawn
sets it adrift and the town breaks loose
from its moorings,
the hubbub of its voices muffled
by the fog's slow tones,
until the beacon's final pronouncements
are washed away in the sea.

Let your heart come here,
an exile in shoes threadbare from wandering
among the dry statements,
the clipped commonplaces,
the sharp local idiom,
until it arrives back at the beginning
practising the lingua franca
of water and salt,
an itinerant receiving the valedictions of the rain,
seeking asylum with the birds,
the assurances of the harsh inhospitable winds.

SPRING IN HENRY STREET

The seasons have gone all awry,
four weeks into spring
we're in winter's strang-
lehold again, on aerials and high

shaky wires starlings trip,
pelted by sudden shrapnel
of hail
they easily lose their grip

in these March weathers,
soft targets the birds
no matter how hard
they puff out their feathers –

for weeks the temperatures have been falling –

and by the canal that drops
from a derelict lock 20 feet down,
the storm's running its icy comb
through the sycamore tops.

It's enought to make you want to join
the bears in their dens, inert,
slack-skinned, but warm
in the mountain's dim still heart.

Daily funerals creep
like black snails along Henry Street,
on the final lap
of someone's trip.

And young women go to the flats
with measured maternal steps
and prams like propagators for seeds
under polythene wraps.

We hear that everywhere ice-
bergs are breaking loose
from the polar caps.
I see them at sunrise

flood-lit by thousands of thousand watt bulbs.
Floating cathedrals
whose stained glass
flanks freely weep

into the arctic seas.
As they drift towards us
the temperatures keep
falling and falling.

Their advance guard
has rounded Black Head.
Something freezing and luminous
glides up Henry Street

leaving seals in its wake
on window sills. No use calling
for help as the temperatures keep falling:
I'm in pack-ice up to my neck.

WHAT HAPPENED TO MADEMOISELLE BOURIENNE?

The attics of great novels are full of them:
older sisters, maiden aunts,
companions to irascible dowager duchesses, governesses,
shy, rouged, spinsterly, frivolous, patient
in coarse hand-mended stockings
their too long waists laced into iron stays
in unbecoming blacks and greys
they creak forever across landings
down back-stairwells
never into drawing-rooms,
awkward, untimely, smelling slightly of must,
reminiscent of night moths
in their lacklustre clumsiness
but passionately attracted to the bright young prince
the dashing officer, the eligible bachelor.

Their ambitions are few:
to be secure and respectable
which only marriage can give.
This they are rarely granted.

Only sometimes
if they have proven themselves worthy
through true obedience, piety and self-denial
they are rewarded with an elderly vicar
who has good connections with the manor and bad breath.
But they will always remain minor characters
in the authorial scheme of things
since there is an endless supply
of wholly disposable women
populating several centuries,

nondescript, of no other particular function
than to throw golden hair, milk white skin
tiny feet, playful girlish laughter, etc. into relief
by wearing an especially ill-fitting dress.

As for Mademoiselle Bourienne,
too pretty for her own good,
too flirtatious for the saturnine author's taste,
she gets dumped after roughly a thousand pages
having neither achieved marriage
to the old prince nor the young.
Be-ribboned foil for the princess' unadorned saintliness
she is left hanging in mid-air
an untidy loose end,
bits of crumpled muslin and lace
sticking out about four-fifths through the novel
like a slightly soiled book-marker.
Obviously the author quite simply
forgot her in the kitchen talking to the cook
or curling her blonde hair with the curling irons
forever enveloped by the smell of singed keratin,
perhaps he left her in the winter-garden
still waiting for Lieutenant Anatole
who died in battle long ago.

Whatever the case may be,
an author who likes to see himself
in the role of a god pre-ordaining fate
or a puppeteer holding all the strings

has fallen down badly
in a case like Mademoiselle Bourienne's,
likeable, fun-loving, entirely
ordinary Mademoiselle Bourienne
who never meant anyone any harm.
She could be married by now,
a plump matron settled in the suburbs of Moscow
with her family and giving her husband
a hand in his furrier's shop.
She could have entered a convent
and died from consumption
or been executed as a spy for Bonaparte.

Let us assume it was a simple mistake,
an oversight,
an entirely ordinary divine oversight.
Lucky for Mademoiselle Bourienne.
Perhaps.

TO THE DISTRIBUTOR OF SOULS

I

With chisel, mallet, drill and blocks of stone
Monk Gislebertus goes to work on souls:
Last Judgement Day on the great tympanum.
Saved or condemned? Left, devils tip the scales
hellwards, right, angels use them as a swing,
a leg-up to the skies. The judge looks out
unmoved from his mandorla. Choirs sing.
Isn't it true to life? Some always miss the boat
and go down screaming. The artist's at his best
portraying the mortal terror of the lost,
the gaping grimace, twisted scowl. The blessed
looked bored to death with joy and all the rest.
It's a tedious story being saved and happy.
Damnation and misery make much better copy.

II

Military glamour
famine appeals
terrestrial tremor
abattoir squeals
long range missile orbits
charity meals
cartoon-like Turkey Shoots

poisoned paddy fields
Fish in a Barrel Shoots
New Asylum Bills
Ducks in Kuwait Shoots
fire-torture grills
total news black-outs
Economic Interest Zones
bodies blown to bits
Rockeye cluster bombs
European Resource Wars
Allied Bomber Jets
commufeminislamic take-over fears
tough marine corps cadets
misery and clamour
carpet sweatshop kids
famine disease and genocide wherever
the US world banker shits.

III

Dear XX,
herewith I am returning my soul.
It needs an overhaul,
the stitching's undone,
the lining is torn,
the bodywork's battered and worn.
The buttons are gone,
the colours have started to run,

I can't control
the shadowy hole
that's obliterating the sun.
I'll throw in the old one without quail
in exchange for a fresh new soul.
the size of a stone
in cherry or plum
and as neat and hard and small.

IV

In the morning
we shake it out
and smooth
its wrinkles.

In the morning
we fold and refold
and – before leaving –
pocket it.

At night we unfold it
shake it out
and – hoping it won't tear –
set sail on the horizon.

At night we unfold it
shake it out
and – praying it won't rip –
parachute into the sky.

V

All night at fever pitch the quarter moon
had trembled like a drink in some glass

which someone raised and slowly downed.
Then dawn came in a night nurse's rustling greys

softly distributing syringes of light,
with graphite pencil sketched the outline of objects,

rumpled sheets, bedside table, bottles and glass,
then washed all watercolours into these,

mixed with some whites for pastel effects,
drained darkness from all corners of the ward,

the windows came unhinged with choice of blues.
Outside the dusty little park slapped shades

of green on and ran riot with the early birds.
The first tram flew around on gleaming rails

and braked and showered the world with sparks.
The sun sent a scout kite over the tops

of the trees before invading the terrain.
Provisionally the experiment was put on hold.

Test tubes tinkled in wooden racks.
Lab coats hung pale as convalescents on their hooks.

VI

Riddle:
Like a woodworm he would crawl
through the roofbeams
of a clean young soul.

VII

You ask for bread,
it gives you iron.
You ask for drink,
it gives you salt water.
You ask for light,
it gives you the new moon.
You ask for rest,
it makes you a bed of thorns.
You ask it to be with you always,
it answers with absence.
You can rely on it.

VIII

The soul millers
are grinding souls.
Dust whispers on roof beams,
on the teeth of cogwheels, on pulleys.
Dust sings in the mill house.
Three watery-eyed women in black:
one whets the stone,
her thumb is broad,
one spins the gold,
her tooth is long,
one uses the blade,
her eye is blunt.
Sisters and brothers
under the juniper tree
did they bury your mothers?
Sisters and brothers
did they make for you
graves of feathers?

IX

We take it off at night
this shapeless garment,
throw it over the back of a chair
and slip into butterfly glamour.

Unbuttoned, unwanted,
limp and grey,
it hangs and waits
knowing it has won the day.

X

You won't believe, he said, what happened to me last night:
My body left my soul. My heart went south looking for a thrill, kissed bottles, the blue moon, guitars, sang in the bars, got drunk and ill and landed in the gutter.
My feet wanted to enter the freemasonry of jackdaws but fell to the ground.
My ears consorted with oysters and clams trying to break into their silent transmissions.
My eyes set their sight on deciphering the code the bark beetle writes on trees or the unending text scripted by swallows and pencilled into the sky with fine black nibs but saw nothing in the dark.
Outside the crickets, the busybodies, shovelled grains of sound into the night's hourglass. What could my poor soul do but wait? There was a picket of bones at my door. Their loudest protestant was my mouth.
When dawn came everything returned, dead-beat, as the earth appeared dressed in green vestments and lawn-sleeves and the birds broke into their shrill matins.
And since then, he said, I feel that something is missing. All day I have been searching for it with my own two hands.

PERMISSIVE DAYS

*For love all love of other sights controls
And makes one little room an everywhere.*
                                John Donne

Given time these awnings widen
On an all-inclusive blue
The glass doors of the day are gliding
Open on a me and you.

As we swing on watered silks
Of a slanting freak horizon
Whereabouts of wharfs and whelks
Breaking wave in whispers spills.

Diligently from your skin
I divine, devise and proffer
How to mouth the slowest tongue
That the planet's got on offer.

If you think we're losing ground
When I kiss your rouges and such
Let the scenery roll round
Concentrate on keeping touch.

Feel the liquor's bottled fire
Jingle-jangle in your throat
Make our room an everywhere
With little room for other thought.

Man your barricades and things
Flag them vivid, flag them red
And watch the tell-tale happenings
Turn mobile feasts upon our bed.

Permissive days worn inside out,
Scenario of our tableaux vivants.
The sun comes up in a Mikado's coat.
Our shoes are filled with moon-lit sands.

NOT A POEM ABOUT WRITING POETRY

For Rita

Sometimes when we meet in loving friendship
under low ceilings or in high dives
drinking from many intoxicating cups,
heads enspiralled by the smoke
of our cigarettes,

we talk of the elevator man in Hungary
who at the time when the frogs nearby in the lake
began their urgent enquiry,
would lift us to the top to the beat of jazz,
keep a symphony orchestra suspended between two floors,

crash into the middle of the drums,
and rise again with trumpets.
When he pressed the buttons
15 passengers flew into an underworld of harmony.
He was like Pluto himself

or an ageing Orpheus
whose song bewitches souls.
He was small and bent, wore a grimy black suit,
and opened his lips on a mellow golden smile.
His face was a little hard to make out like a god's.

On 3 by 5 feet, for half a minute or so
he held our lives in his hand,
ferried us lightly while the cogwheels turned.
Coming to a stop he'd open the door,
dance aside and give out bouquets of violins.

You say: 'Do you remember the old guy with his radio
in the elevator in Debrecen? Did you ever write
that poem about him?' I did not,' I reply,
'and I doubt that I ever will.'
We both think of him as still rising to a perfect pitch.

GOAT

I

Acrobats of the mountainside
high-stepping over the top
at dawn
horns wound with streamers of light.

II

No one knows like a goat
the rock's most secret chemistry
its veins of frozen salt.

III

The goat's favourite foods:
young leaves of the silver ash
the oak, birch and plantain
all types of ivy, sage, oregano
wild thyme and henbane
and every 30 days or so
it devours the whole of the moon.

IV

A body of lancets and angles,
knobs, protrusions and points
and tapered joints,
ribs, pelvis and spine
arranged into one strong sweep of the neck

and gathered together in the skull's
austere gothic design.

V

Prometheus chose the goat
as friend and helpmate.
Its eyes stare proudly
from their background of glazed gold:
stolen fire set them alight;
they have seen gods defied.

VI

What tossing of beards and locking of horns
when two rivals contend –
belligerent old men
in a parliament.

VII

The goat is horny.
The goat stinks.
The goat is capricious.
The goat is greedy.
The goat is sinful.
The goat has sex with his daughters.
It's all the goat's fault.
Let's sacrifice him to Apollo
to Priapus
to Venus
to Jehova.
Let's banish him into the desert.
Let's send him down to hell.

VIII

If two helices appear over a stonewall,
there's no need to be frightened
unless it's a midday in high summer
and they're accompanied by the sound of a reed pipe.

IX

When Böcklin painted Pan
lurking between sedge and rush
he used a few tied-together bristles
from Pan's tail as a brush.

X

He who drinks the wind.
He who breathes through his ears.
He who dreams like a human.
He who begets male offspring when the wind is southerly,
female when it comes from the North.

XI

When two goats meet on a narrow bridge
over deep water
one of them will kneel down
to allow the other
stride over it and across.

XII

Goat's meat, if sautéd, then baked in honey
spiced with bayleaves
and served in a vinegar sauce
is a powerful medicine
against epilepsy.
Ashes of a goat's horns
cure sleeping sickness;
mixed with oil of myrrh
they prevent heart disease
and underarm smells.
Ashes of a goat's hooves
are used against an inflamed anus
and loss of hair.
The blood is potent in a variety of ways:
Pulverize it, mix it with the powder
of dried octopus,
pepper, thyme and wine
and it heals
all conceivable ills.

XIII

A goat was wetnurse and mother to Zeus.
Now a cluster of stars
perched on the brink of the skies
she looks down nightly
with glittering eyes.

XIV

Look at him in the bars
all girls and silken cigars
and girls and tequila
girls and guitars
gold rings and fast cars –
macho cabrillo.

XV

A kid will be a certain winner
as present for your host
at dinner,

it is also a popular first prize
in poetry or singing competitions
otherwise

you might give one to your spouse
as token of gratitude and love,
very cheap at only half an Obolus

when it takes one to pay the ferryman
to take you across the river Styx:
greedy coal-eyed Charon.

XVI

I was raised in a city far from goats.
I didn't know their perfectly tailored
coats that fitted them closely
cut from rough brown fabric
with a bluish velvet stripe down the spine,
I didn't know their hooves carved
from basalt,

nor their buff horns streaked
with dirty yellow little streaks in the ridges
from just below the points
down to the frontal nubs whence they grew,
I didn't know they walked with mincing steps
like courtly ladies
and that their black lacquered pupils
were horizontal slots
for the small coins of a summer day,
I didn't know any of this,
but one day climbing in the mountains
when I was twelve
and the heat made the outlines
of fields and firs and rocky peaks
tremble and shiver around me,
a goat crossed my path
calling, I thought, to me to follow.
With its colourful horns
it pushed open a door
into the cool darkness of a well house
where from a rusty pipe
water was running
that came straight from the heart
of the mountain –
ice-cold and more delicious
than I ever knew water could be.

XVII

When the dead finally rise
take off their goat skins
masks and horns
wipe the blood from their faces
and go to their homes
you'll know that for the time being at least
the tragedy has ended.

GLASGOW AUBADE

Early June in a Glasgow guesthouse,
a morning that yellows like old newspapers,
old lace, or the Victorian
sandstone façades on Renfrew Street,

and we, half-asleep still in the oyster-pale air,
are suddenly waterborne,
waterbound,
our ears awash with the lick and lap of water.

Next-door someone is up,
running the tap,
until the wall behind our heads is filled
with water music

starting with a ping, ping, ping,
a trickle of notes
as though an instrument were being tuned,
the pizzicato of an off-key string
being plucked and tightened,

then a steadier stream of sound,
distant at first but closing in on us
like a marching band
passing or the onset of wood winds
picking up a theme
in spurts, high-pitched and clear,

a cantus firmus to the deep
sweet cistern song,
its basso continuo fluent and meandering
through a system of last century's lead pipes,
copper-joints, bends and gaskets,

a basin that receives and swallows
and carries away in its culvert
the night's grit and dust,
the wreckage of sleep,
until fluidity is everywhere
and we step into this changeable river,
half-dreaming drift in its shallows,

ponds, water-meadows shimmy and tango
with spider-like insects,
a fleet of ships gravely
slips out of sight
on long silent oars.

This is a morning of the first water.
It rises and lifts us like flotsam
until we awake on the back of an ocean
that sings,

trusting its give and take
its continuous swell and surge
will beach us gently in this day,
in this room where the last high tide
has left its mark
way above our heads.

SUMMER NEAR AUVERS

> *"Exaggerate the essentials ... "*
> Vincent Van Gogh

At midday near Auvers, that's exactly what the sun does:
like the painter's brush it runs riot
over the thunderstruck yellows of these vast fields,

flocks of crows are there, too, gathering
in troubled skies, the bones of flight and hunger
laid bare by a few decisive black strokes.

The sky is unchanged; it's now as then like a heavy
blue jar or a tin into which he squeezed the remains
from various tubes: woad, cobalt, bitumen,

and the same cicadas still give their humdrum
running commentaries, thousands of small grey sticks
hammering the empty drum of midday.

Dark paths beaten through the wheat in deep ruts
cut in from beyond the framed countryside, from Arles,
Paris or further north from Groot-Zundert perhaps

and from beyond today, this summer or even century:
deadlines stopping us in our tracks
reminding us how little time is left.

FROM CORRESPONDENCE SECRÈTE

for Hermann Rasche

Frankfurt am Main,

My dear friend,

I feel such an urge to write to you
at this moment, the others are at church,
so I don't have to be afraid
of being interrupted
for they must never know about this letter.

Since Johann Wolfgang left for Leipzig
everyone has changed towards me.
My parents admonish me daily
to take more interest in my appearance and cooking,
Father has locked away the books
Johann Wolfgang and I used to read together –
Voltaire, Racine, Lessing
and my beloved Klopstock –
I am denied all writing materials
since last Saturday when he found me
with pen and paper in the sewing room.
Don't ask me where I got them for this
and how I will bribe the maid
to smuggle it out of the house.

Johann Wolfgang's letters have become
very different, very didactic
in tone. He pontificates. He tells me:

"you little girls cannot see
as far ahead as we poets".
He's hardly more than a year older than I,
we were taught the same things,
read the same books and yet he gives me orders:
don't read novels, don't study philosophy,
learn languages instead,
the ins and outs of house-keeping.
He has forbidden me the Decameron,
Mahomet and Pitaval,
saying that this kind of enlightenment
is not meant for me "but for a man who is able
to reflect on these items and events."

I know very well what this is all about.
A woman with masculine knowledge
is spoilt for a man,
and I must eventually be married,
for living as a spinster in my parents' house
would be intolerable for me.

What an advantage beauty is!
Men prefer it to the charm
of soul and mind.
And if we can't be pretty or bewitching
like Lisette who threw forty young men's hearts
off balance at the last ball
we must at least provide a dowry
and a pleasant home.
I fear no man will ever love me
for I am growing uglier every day.
Say what you like, dear friend,
my mirror doesn't lie.

If only my father would let me study as I want
someone might find me bearable then.
There must be another Charles Grandison
who can see
beneath the unattractive surface!
And yet although a loveless marriage of convenience
fills me with abject horror
it is the only way open to me.

Ah chère amie,
I would give everything to match
the excellence of Miss Byron.
But this dull and monotonous life
and the sadness that rarely lifts from my soul
have destroyed my burning wish to write ...
Johann Wolfgang is fast becoming famous
celebrating his first literary and erotic triumphs.
He has forgotten about his sister,
our days spent reading and talking together.
He never writes to me now that he's got Charlotte.

I will be engaged to a man called Schlosser,
whose presence fills me with revulsion
but I will die young perhaps
from complications during childbirth
as so frequently happens.

I am not yet twenty and I have nothing else
to look forward to in this world
and no one to turn to except you,
dear friend, whom I hardly know.
    I kiss and embrace you
    Cornelia G.

THE SCRAP DEALER'S REPORT

After the fifth summer of earthquakes and floods,
when typhoid fever raged in the city,
the people gathered behind the cemetery wall
and without much talk moved into the centre
smashing every statue on the way,
they hacked and sawed them apart,
rid the squares of heroes, gestures of triumph,
hands reaching for the sky.

It was a toned-down finale,
a quick and sober tidying-up action,
and all that's left from the march of progress
is the iron boot,
footless and forgotten on the pedestal.

Where are they now,
the flaming mock suns of ideals,
fireworks of hope,
pretty optical illusions?

For us scrap dealers things are tough.
Our yards are filling up
with arms, legs, cracked skulls,
everywhere you turn, the stare
of battered gigantic faces.

But we are biding our time
because it is sure to come:
the people need idols
and we'll sell them cheap.

However, we promise no miracles,
water into wine, loafs and fishes
sort of hocus pocus.
There will never be enough bread to go round,
water will stay water for most,
wine wine for the few,
and from now on it's every man for himself.

READING HIKMET IN CONNEMARA
Autumn '95

for Corinna, Jürgen & Hannes

Stiller than usual, these September days
arrived without circumstance,
showed true colours on rocks and Twelve Bens
and the horseshoe-shaped twin bays.

At the pier a flotilla of boats
loaded up a cargo of sunlight
ripe as melons, and the sun was tied
to the fishing nets as a float.

On powerlines a conference of starlings
held their agitated plenary debate,
chug-chug went a trawler setting out
and a slow breath was rising and falling.

Just the hint of a surge on the strand
like the crackle and long swish of a dress,
the frou-frou of silk fizzled out, a splash,
a crab sidled over the sand.

On the stonewall next to the turnstile
a herring-gull presided over the dunes
with the air of a sovereign in exile
staring vacantly at the scene.

In the graveyard beyond the wall
grass lay matted like hair on the ground,
the crosses were tilted and leaning,
three times rang the curlew's call

and three score more times and again,
you could set your watch by it.
Not a breeze; the fields were quiet
except for a donkey's braying.

Open-handed the country received us,
came with its largesse to the door
of shells and flowers, blackberries
paid sweet lip-service to peace.

"The most beautiful sea's the one
not yet travelled" goes a line
in one of Nâzim Hikmet's love poems
which I read during that time.

I found the great Turkish poet
wedged between Russell and Bloch,
between rationalism and hope
was a good spot for him, I thought,

neither would he look out of place here
taking hay (to his cattle) on his back,
repairing the motor on his curragh
or having a smoke by the pier.

Nâzim, singer of love songs,
despite twenty-odd years in jail,
his heart kept time within stone walls
"announcing each dawn like a gong".

The head and the heart stay the same,
no matter what happens, he said,
he never gave up or in,
how his fire still sets me aflame.

Our times seem to have grown indifferent,
or is it we who've grown cynical and old
with nothing to sing or hope for
at a freezing cold century's end?

But there are fires on the hillsides today
and the sun has heated up the rocks;
the air is so clear. I look
at the beautiful untravelled sea.

TRIP TO AN ISLAND

for Eoin

I

We crossed valley after valley,
overcame mountain passes, made shortcuts
from headland to headland
pushing their foreshores out into the open-
armed Atlantic till we couldn't go further
West, at the end of a pier we embarked

on a little ship which, moored
with blue ropes, steadily rose and fell.
I fancied I rode
on the back of a large breathing mammal,
swaying it lifted and put us down again gently
and finally the ship was untied from the quay

by boys with nautical skills, they loosened
knots, long-jumped aboard split-seconds
after the craft had been
thrown one last time against buffers,
black tractor tyres lining the wall,
and quickly the full-blown sea

invaded our bodies, our minds, we thought
in fathoms and leagues, its ups and downs
entered us, we recommended
our souls to the ferryman who did balancing acts
in the wheel house washed out in denims,
his transistor played waltzes,

waves fell onto the deck, we swung
to and fro, a fine spray blew
smoke from our cigarettes,
a flask made the rounds against sea-sickness
and chill, all round us maritime birds,
cormorants, herring-gulls, kittiwakes,

engaged in outrageous flying manoeuvres passed
and repassed us, skimmed the turbulent surface, dived
it seemed, for our sole enjoyment,
scores of jelly fish reeled in the water
like animated flowers, we sailed
around outposts of rock strictly in keeping

with the fairway, the island approached us
with luminous fields, its high mole
lobsterpot-piled, the crescent
of a white strand rose, the ruin of the pirate
queen's fortress and behind it the only
mountain peak – deep in clouds. Disembarking

we looked back at the land we had left
on the horizon, a dark strip of rock
from a past we knew less about
or were rapidly forgetting, and I saw with relief
how lucky our trip had been, so far not one of us
had been turned into a pillar of salt.

II

The bed and breakfast belongs to an ex-lumberjack recently
returned from Canada, red-bearded he juggles
eggs and bacon in his bachelor's kitchen, serves us

what passes for tea in his house so black
and sweet it sends your mind reeling,
"That'll put hair on your chest, Missus", he jokes

standing in his rock-strewn frontgarden, wind-
tousled and hungover he directs us to the beach
on the southern tip of the island.

"10,000 years ago you could have walked
from the top of the mountain
to Paris and back without getting your feet wet",

he says encouragingly as parting shot.
Following the track through water-logged fields we pass
under the mountain's great cliff face, keep

to the fault-line which runs
through the island and then continues under the sea
to other islands, other continents.

Down at the beach we find the tide has gone out
further past the rocks that lie like a herd
of sea cattle with rounded backs,

shining wet, garlanded with slimy kelp
and pock-marked with limpets clinging on
for dear life. Two people gather periwinkles,

moving slowly along the strand
in darkblue corporation jackets,
patches of oil-cloth on shoulders and elbows

glisten black as they bend down and rise,
up and down, as though saying their prayers
to an island divinity.

The shallows between the rocks are blue
and clear and each wave that rolls in
and pulls out again with its own peculiar moan

is shot through by thousands of splinters,
glassneedles, shoals of young fry. In the rockpools
green fur grows and strange tree-like

stalks with segmented spines. A thing floats, half
jellied bulb, half suction dredge, and having
tunnelled itself out a little crab shakes crooked

shears free of sand, cranks up its hydraulic chassis
and sets to work picking over bones
that have long been picked clean.

And above all glides a black-headed gull,
swoops and strikes through the blue air
and takes the updraught, circles, glides

and circles again – a bit of a show-off, we think –
comes to a complete standstill for a few seconds
when everything seems to hang in the balance –

a hiatus which includes
sea, shore, rocks, grass, distant mountains, sky,
winkle pickers, hunters and hunted

and us too who stand motionless, wishing
this momentary reprieve could last forever
until the gull strikes anew

hitting its target precisely,
and although we have seen all this before
we don't know whether to laugh or cry.

III

Imagine fields as text
and you could read these furrows,
these lazy-beds under their sodden rush-lined covers
word by word
and sentence by sentence
as an island people's epic.

Every noun or verb unearthed,
turned over again and again
in the harsh light of hunger,
repeats the same intelligence
inscribed with the coarsest of tools
spade, rake or hoe, into the soil.

You can hear the heavy beat
the dactyls and trochees
of ploughing and digging,
of the whole back-breaking labour
doubled over wrist-deep in wet clay,
moving up and down the beds

from morning till nightfall
season after season
until standing up straight
is a forgotten art. These
are the rhythms that informed
the island's history,

shaped it into ripples,
ruts, corrugations,
a country like whipcord
undulating and green under our feet
and not an inch of ground
that doesn't bear the imprint

of a human hand,
leaving us this narrative,
chapter and verse
of hardship and exile and yet –
if you read between the lines –
also of courage and trust.

Nothing illuminates the manuscript
of these fields, except perhaps
where the alchemist sun lights up
strips of gold in a drainage ditch
or in spring when the earth throws up
masses of narcissi, irises, lilies.

IV

Around here silence is rare
because no one turns off
the sad old drone, the sea;

the wind whistles chants,
lingering on all their sharps and flats
and the waves roll up like emigrants in transit

reluctant to unpack frayed scarves
that have seen grander days,
brown fancy skirts in shreds,

toss polished stones, shells,
their hoarded bric-a-brac into the surf
until the tide pulls them out

before they can disclose the cool
treasures, the beautiful grotesques
moving in their depths.

But it can happen that one day
walking along the tidal line
you find a sea urchin on the sand

panoplied with limegreen spikes
a fin-de-siècle fruit
plucked by a freak undertow and dropped

before your feet on a grey island morning.
You pick it up and wonder
how compact and heavy it is

smelling of fish and decay
and out of its depth in all this air and light
where the wind lingers on its sharps and flats

and the homeless waves rock and roll
to the drone of the sea.
So you throw it back

into the water that gave it
a rare offering
a gift you'll always remember in your palms.

V

Rock has the undisputed monopoly
expanding its freehold
until the whole world turns to stone.
Which came first here,

you're tempted to ask,
stone or the word for it
in the vocabulary of barrenness
picked up from the ground

and laid along boundaries
till a network of clauses,
a lapidary syntax,
was flung over the island,

stones stained by the rust,
the black or white inks,
the grey washes of lichens,
some stamped with the fossilized

imprint of a fern,
a fish skeleton or marine shell,
lifted and piled waist-high into walls
around field giving on field

like turns of phrase
and paraphrase following each other
in the idiom of toil
and fatigue

held together by the conjunction of hands
that pass on stone after stone
to build structures
a child could knock a breach into,

loosely joined to one another
allowing for breathing space,
as words in a sentence
are loosely joined

with an "and", "but" or "nevertheless",
by makeshift gates,
wooden planks, car doors,
the top of an old brass bed,

but constructed
with a careful eye to balance and function,
to allowing air and light
pass through unhindered

and, most difficult of all, to the art
of using the materials provided,
no matter how poor,
in all best possible ways,

doing what is needed most
at any given time and with good grace.

VI

In the long bright nights of summer
When the sun, the luminary,
Lolling on its western divan
Makes light work of lighthouse beacons,

When the moon, the hornèd vassal,
Gently whitens summer ditches
Overgrown with cress and rushes,
Polishes the five-mile stonewall

Looping up and round the commonage
Where the earnest sheep are cropping
Fields to springy velvet turf;
Here in daytime from the clifftop

You can see the wind do tangos
On a vast blue ballroom floor,
Swirl the salty spray so high up
You might think you had your face slapped

By the waves' wet underclothing;
In these dusky summer midnights
Leaning over gates and stonewalls
Feet at rest on summer flowers –

Cranesbills, daisies, and white orchids
And the purple pads of wild thyme –
Stand the old men of the island,
Gentle-spoken in their tweed caps,

They discuss the world situation,
And the fishing before Diesel,
Talk of letters by their children,
News from Birmingham and Boston,

And the time when Maureen Brady
Left the island for her first trip
Across the ocean to her brother
In the South of England whom she

Hadn't seen for twenty years.
How she came back two weeks later
With his ashes in a clay urn,
How a neighbour brought the ashes

Out one evening in his curragh
Scattered them across the water
As she knew her brother'd wished.
Thus the old men talk all hours

In the mild midsummer night
Leaning over gates and stonewalls;
Accordions in the pub play louder
And the foxglove scents grow stronger,

All the windows stand wide open,
Stars shoot down the slide and vanish,
New ones slip into their places.
Did the Great Bear not for seconds

Open one green blinking eye?
Or was it a transatlantic
Greeting from a passing Jumbo?
Boats are pulled up on the foreshore,

Oars tugged well in on the bottoms,
Lie at rest between the heaps of
Green and orange nylon fishnets,
Like your hand palm-up beside me on the sheet.

NOTES

THE ANNUNCIATION
Val d'Arbia is an area in Tuscany not far from Siena. In various cultures the owl was considered as harbinger of death.

TO THE DISTRIBUTOR OF SOULS
Gislebertus, sculptor of the tympanum on the romanesque cathedral of St Lazare at Autun in Burgundy. Turkey – fish in barrel – ducks in Kuwait shoots – all descriptions of the killing of Iraqi soldiers and civilians by American army personnel during the second Gulf War.

GOAT
According to South American Indian folk legend the moon wanes because a goat is eating it. The actors of Greek tragedies originally wore goat skins, masks and horns, hence "tragedy" from "tragos", i.e. male goat.

SUMMER NEAR AUVERS
"Vast fields under troubled skies": Van Gogh's own description of this series of paintings painted not long before his suicide in Auvers-sur-Oise on September 27, 1890. "Exaggerate the essentials" is a quote from one of his letters to his brother Theo on painting technique. Groot Zundert is his place of birth in Northern Brabant.

FROM CORRESPONDENCE SECRÈTE
This poem is to some extent a montage of direct quotes from the secret letters, or Correspondence Secrète, written by Cornelia Goethe (1750-1777), sister of the German poet Johann Wolfgang von Goethe (1749-1832). For this I am indebted to an article by Dr. Hermann Rasche, UCG, about "Cornelia Goethe's short unhappy life."

READING HIKMET IN CONNEMARA
Nazim Hikmet (1902-1963), Turkish poet, repeatedly tried and sentenced for his left-wing political convictions. In 1938 he was condemned to 29 years solitary confinement. After his release in 1951 he lived in Moscow.